Contents

Families everywhere

Families live all over the world.
Every family is different.

parents

grandparents

children

A family is a group of people who are related to each other.

Different types of families

Some families are big.

Some families are small.

Some families live together.

Some families live far apart.

Sometimes people in a family look a bit like each other.

Sometimes two families join together to make one family.

What do families do?

Families look after each other.

Families help each other.

Some families work together.

Some families play together.

Some families exercise together.

Some families look after pets together.

Some families celebrate festivals together.

Some families travel together.

Families are everywhere.

Who is in your family?

Map of families around the world

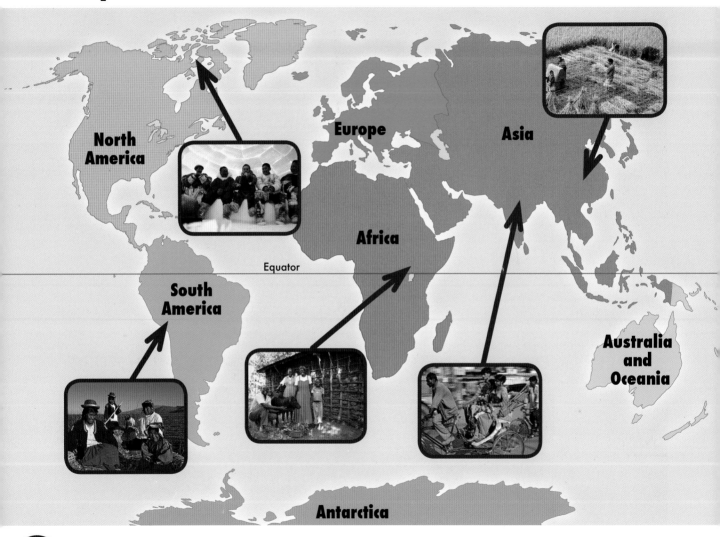

North America

Europe

Asia

Africa

Equator

South America

Australia and Oceania

Antarctica

Picture glossary

exercise do an activity that helps you stay healthy

festival special time for a group of people

Index

Notes for parents and teachers
Before reading
Show children the cover of the book and read the title. Then turn to the contents page. With the children, read the entries on the contents page and explain that this is a tool to help readers know what information is in the book and where to find it. Ask children to predict what they will learn from this book after reading the table of contents.

After reading
- Turn to page 5 and discuss how labels are used with the picture to identify different members of the family. Have children name other types of family members (aunt, uncle, cousin, etc.). Then, have them draw a picture of their own family and label the family members.
- Discuss how this book has examples of families from all over the world. Discuss how there are many similarities with families, no matter where they live. Have children look at the photo on page 4. Then, point out the map on page 22. Demonstrate for children how to use the map to identify that the photo on page 4 was taken in South America.

Note on picture on page 19 & 22: NEVER ride a bicycle without a helmet.